Winning the week now:
Planning a productive week daily

Joseph L. Smith,

Copyright page

All rights reserved. No part of this publication may be reproduced, distributed, or transmitted in any form or by any means, including photocopying, recording, or other electronic or mechanical methods, without the prior written permission of the publisher, except in the case of brief quotations embodied in critical reviews and certain other noncommercial uses permitted by copyright law.
Copyright ©Joseph L. Smith, 2022.

TABLE OF CONTENT

Introduction

Chapter One:instructions to eliminate the protection from winning the week

Chapter Two:We use the resolution to finish stuff.

Chapter Three:step-by-step instructions to designate opportunities to supply

Chapter Four:the most effective method to execute your arrangement

Chapter Five:How Do I Create a Plan And Stick To It

Chapter Six:instructions to quit diverting yourself

Chapter Seven: stop outer interruptions

Chapter Eight:investigate your mentality

Introduction

Week by week arranging is the method involved with putting together your objectives and needs for the week ahead. Figuring out how to design your week assists you with dealing with your time better and guarantees you start every week feeling engaged and useful.

Arranging your week ahead of time saves time, supports efficiency, and assists you with accomplishing more. At the point when you plan your week on a Friday or Sunday, you get coordinated and assume command over your time permitting you to make a move on your greatest needs for the week on Monday morning.

Figuring out how to design your week assists you with explaining your most significant work and permits you to make a point-by-point rundown of the activity steps expected to accomplish your week-after-week objectives. Week by week arranging disposes of interruption and overpowering and assists you with working on your concentration and consideration.

Making clear week after week anticipates the impending week will assist you with remaining coordinated and in charge of your time. At the point when you really plan your week really, you'll begin your week with deliberateness as opposed to stressing over what you ought to do.

In this part, I'll share 6 hints on the most proficient method to design your week really so you can foster a superior week-after-week work plan. These week-after-week arranging tips will assist you with feeling clear, fit, and certain about recognizing and making a move on your greatest week-after-week needs.

Step-by-step instructions to design your week
The following are 6 weeks after week arranging tips.

1. Survey your drawn-out plans
At the point when you don't design your week given your objectives, you will not be as compelling. While arranging your week, begin with a survey of your long-haul and transient objectives. Get clear on where you are presently and what progress you need to make before the week's over.

Explaining what progress you need to make guarantees you invest your energy every week on your most significant and useful errands. At the point when you are sure about your objectives, it's simpler to list a couple of activity steps or ventures you want to zero in on for the impending week. This cycle saves investment.

Utilize your drawn-out objectives to lay out five quantifiable objectives you need to accomplish for that week.

2. Plan your week on a Sunday

To design your week successfully, make a timetable each Sunday night for the impending week. Track down a tranquil spot in a quiet climate and endure ten to fifteen minutes arranging your week.

Arranging your week on a Sunday guarantees you start each Monday early daytime feeling engaged and useful. At the point when you plan your week on a Sunday, you can commit significant time on a Monday morning to make a move on your most significant work.

Week after week arranging guarantees you don't stress over what to do or where to contribute your experience on a Monday. Arranging your week on a Sunday removes you from the present and assists you with explaining the outcomes you need to accomplish before the week's over without the pressure of playing make up for lost time.

Allowing yourself to design your week ahead of time will save long periods of sitting around idly. Assuming you like, use Friday evening to prepare.

3. Put forth your week-by-week boundaries
Arranging your week ahead of time allows you an opportunity to lay out your boundaries for the week so you can raise a ruckus around town running on Monday morning. While laying out week after week boundaries, audit your greater plans and objectives to guarantee that your week-by-week needs line up with your drawn-out vision.

Begin by making a rundown of all that you need to finish that week. Then, take a gander at everything and settle on your four or five greatest needs for the week. On the off chance that you plan your week yet neglect to focus, you won't know where to begin.

Distinguishing your needs for the week will explain the results you need to accomplish, which will assist you with dealing with your time better and increment your efficiency.

4. Plan your week in a timetable
When you are sure about your needs for the week, you can plan your most significant errands. While arranging your day guarantee you pause for a minute to plan the needs that will assist you with accomplishing your week-by-week objectives.

Having your week-after-week plan on a paper organizer, week-by-week arranging application, or post-it notes will assist you with dealing with your daily agenda. This guarantees you shut out the opportunity to chip away at your week-by-week needs.

Planned errands make you more useful and guarantee that you generally make a move on the needs that make the biggest difference. At the point when you plan your time, you know where to contribute your time for the greatest outcomes which dispose of interruption and increments center.

5. Construct your week-after-week schedule
When you plan your week after week plan, make useful propensities and schedules to assist you with accomplishing your week after week objectives. Making week after week schedules gives guidance, and center, and diminishes pressure.

To make your week-after-week schedule, begin by illustrating the exercises you can do to further develop your efficiency consistently. Begin by making a rundown of the things you need to finish every day. You can likewise acquaint yourself with a night schedule with audit your day-to-day and week-after-week progress.

Your week-by-week schedule could remember enjoying standard reprieves or working for lumps of time. It may very well be more useful for you to bunch comparable errands together or to go for a long stroll during the day to keep your energy high.

Begin by building two or three efficiency propensities into your day-to-day plan. When you have accomplishments with them, integrate these propensities into your customary week-by-week schedule.

6. Audit your week-by-week progress
The most ideal way to design your week is to get some margin to audit your week. Having a week-after-week survey is a potential chance to consider the previous week, plan for the week ahead, and guarantee your plan for the day lines up with your objectives.

Surveying your week is additionally an amazing chance to commend your accomplishments, audit your advancement, and distinguish any snags that are keeping you down. A week-by-week survey assists you with understanding how you're effectively planning your financial time. It additionally lays the right foundation for defining your boundaries for the next week.

Getting some margin to survey your week-after-week designs expands certainty, inspiration, and force.

Summarizing
Arranging your week ahead of time brings down pressure and expands your efficiency. At the point when you plan your week, guarantee you set aside some margin to survey greater plans, put forth your boundaries, and make your timetable for the week.

Arranging your week ahead of time guarantees you start the week feeling engaged and useful. Week by week arranging likewise provides you more noteworthy heading and motivation, guaranteeing you know precisely where to contribute your time, energy, and concentration.

Chapter One: instructions to eliminate the protection from winning the week

Have you at any point attempted to roll out an improvement in your life — a positive one, enhancing, and useful — however, face your foolish ways of behaving?

Perhaps you chose to begin working out, eating great, or resting better, yet you felt a sense of urgency to act in manners that undermined those objectives. Or on the other hand, you postponed, procrastinated, and tried not to do things you knew would improve your life, until you stalled out, surrendered, or wanted to have some time off.

In conducting brain research, we refer to this peculiarity as "opposition."

Obstruction is an innate attribute of progress. It's an obstruction we're probably going to confront whether our ideal change is little (like drinking an additional glass of water in the first part of the day) or huge (like stopping smoking or beginning a new position).

Notwithstanding its shared characteristic, the opposition keeps on astonishing, disappointing, and puzzles a large number of our earnest attempts to change. Whenever left uncontrolled, besides the fact that opposition can make the change cycle harder than it should be, it can likewise disrupt your good-natured endeavors and leave you feeling disappointed.

Anyway, what precisely is the opposition? Also, how might we conquer opposition?

Man Rings Exercise

What Is "Obstruction" Anyway?

Most importantly, the opposition is a mental response to change. It resembles a self-insurance instrument where we go against the change or battle against our ideal change in conduct. That's what the opposition intends, despite being exceptionally energetic with the best goals, we battle that change at a mental level.

To make the cycle more troublesome, we may not know about our obstruction since it happens at a psyche level. For some individuals, the opposition can feel like an unseen conflict between two pieces of ourselves — one that needs to change and one that secretly battles it. This undercover opposition can feel like an internal revolutionary (or an irritating baby who persistently says, "no").

Notwithstanding the mental reaction, the opposition can likewise be a physiological response. Since the change interaction requires additional work, energy, and mental ability, obstruction can incite actual sensations of uneasiness like sleepiness, laziness, and ease back development designs.

At the point when we gather the mental and physiological parts of opposition into a single unit, we frequently see conduct and profound states, for example,

Hesitation
Fooling around
Rationalizing
Evasion
Interruption
Postponing
Hairsplitting
Dormancy and feeling stuck
Overthinking or loss of motion by-investigation
Destructive behavior
Low inspiration and mind-set
Enjoying some time off from change (notwithstanding just barely beginning)
Surrendering or tumbling off the cart

Eventually, we've all accomplished protection from change. I've felt it hundreds — if not thousands — of times and perceive a significant number of the above ways of behaving in myself.

All in all, if protection from change is a typical encounter, for what reason does it work out, and for what reason does it feel awkward? How about we investigate neuroscience for certain responses?

The new source of inspiration
3 Important Bits of Neuroscience if You Want to Overcome Resistance
1. The Prefrontal Cortex
At the point when we experience a novel, new thing, unique, or uncommon, the prefrontal cortex region of our mind illuminates. This piece of the cerebrum processes thoughts, insights, and strategies and is profoundly energy-serious — it can handle a specific measure of information at once to rapidly weariness. In this way, when we experience change, whether or not the change is

positive or negative, our mind needs to work harder.

2. The Amygdala

The additional work and handling power expected by our prefrontal cortex to explore change can likewise animate mental and actual distress. This inconvenience can then enact a piece of our mind called the amygdala. The amygdala is liable for our "battle, flight, freeze" reaction to stress, risk, and the unexplored world. At the point when initiated, this piece of our cerebrum can invigorate sensations of dread and outrage and influence us to act genuinely and imprudently. It can likewise incite mental states like disavowal, disarray, gloom, and emergency.

3. The Basal Ganglia

Conversely, our current schedules and regular propensities are put away in our basal ganglia. Our ways of behaving are profoundly implanted in this piece of our mind. The basal ganglia computerized our considerations, ways of behaving, and activities at an oblivious level, so these things are profoundly proficient and require little exertion and energy to process.

This makes sense of why we normally will generally oppose change — besides the fact that change requires the prefrontal cortex part of our cerebrum to work harder, it likewise causes mental and profound uneasiness and politeness of the amygdala. It's nothing unexpected then that our body's normal reaction is to oppose change and return to the wellbeing of business as usual, securely put away in the energy-effective basal ganglia.

The most effective method to Overcome Resistance (and Get What You Want in Life)

Different Factors That Contribute to Resistance Past the neuroscience, different variables can add to uplifted degrees of obstruction. These middle around the course of progress and the changing climate — at the end of the day, how the change was presented and what else was going on at that point.

For instance, beneath are a few contributing variables I've encountered that expanded my opposition levels:

Presenting changes excessively fast, so I felt overpowered and my cerebrum said "no."
Not completely focusing on the change, for example doing it to satisfy others as opposed to doing it for myself.
Underrating how hard change was and misjudging my capacity to deal with it.
Not understanding how tacky the propensity was that I needed to change.
The outpouring impact, for example, the unexpected effect change had on different pieces of my life.
Startling outer variables, similar to the response of others, the impact of other life-altering situations, work issues, or social elements.

Felt genuinely associated with my "old" conduct and did not figure out why that association was an area of strength to do so.

Absence of help systems and feeling like I ought to have the option to change without assistance.

Feeling of dread toward the obscure and apprehension about rehashing a pessimistic encounter, expanded sensations of stress and overpowering.

You could perceive yourself in a portion of the above-mentioned. Assuming this is the case, I have uplifting news — while we can't change our mind's science (at any rate, not temporarily), we can alter different elements that influence our obstruction levels.

Given that, I'm sharing my five-step cycle to perceive, make due, and defeat obstruction.

My 5-Step Process to Overcome Resistance

Stage 1: Expect Resistance

Opposition makes certain to happen eventually in the change cycle, so tolerating that probability and monitoring the signs is a major initial step.

Take a stab at making a rundown of the kinds of opposition you've encountered before, similar to stalling, destructive behavior, overpowering, sluggishness, or needing to surrender. Keep that rundown convenient and apparent, so when you begin to feel obstruction sneaking in, you can see and see the truth about it.

Stage 2: Prepare for Obstacles
The opposition will increment decisively even with surprising hindrances. Hence, plan and get ready for things that could impede your ideal change.

For instance, to begin strolling first thing, a couple of deterrents might wreck that change, for example, the climate, late evenings, early work gatherings, diseases, and others' activities. Making arrangements for those obstructions — and having procedures set up to manage them — will significantly lessen my degrees of opposition.

Stage 3: Remember Your "Why"

It may very well be simple, during the time spent changing, to lose all sense of direction in the subtleties or make up for the lost time in the progression of life's occupied ness. We here and there fail to remember why we need to change, why it's essential to us, and how it benefits us.

To counter this, record the advantages of progress and the detriments of not evolving. This turns into your "why" and is a convincing motivation to direct you through the most elevated levels of opposition. Place that convincing explanation someplace apparent and help yourself to remember it frequently. For instance, stick a note on the cooler, storage space entryway, or washroom mirror, or make it the screensaver on your cell phone.

To make your "why," have a go at noting the beneath prompts:

What will occur assuming that I do change?
What will occur if I don't change?

What will not occur assuming I change?
What will not occur if I don't change?
The most effective method to Overcome Resistance (and Get What You Want in Life)

Stage 4: Build Your Support Team
As we probably are aware at this point, change can feel hard. Furthermore, when obstruction strikes, it very well may be enticing to attempt to manage it without anyone else. In any case, using others' insight into progress can be important.

Thus, before you start, lay out who your encouraging group of people will be — it may very well be a confided-in companion, partner, online gathering, or in-person group. Utilize this encouraging group of people to share your battles, conceptualize, and gain from their experience.

Note: If you've partaken in the Whole Life Challenge, you'll know how priceless help can be in the changing venture. Whether it's through a group, the WLC Facebook bunch, or the overall impressions of thousands of players, the information, experience, and backing inside the Challenge people group is tremendous. My recommendation is to use that design and offer your experience — you should rest assured others have confronted your obstruction previously or are going through a comparative encounter now.

Stage 5: Learn and Adjust
Each time we experience obstruction, we have a valuable chance to gain from it. Instead of being baffled by our opposing ways or critical of our capacities, we can utilize the change interaction as an opportunity for growth.

Reflect and survey frequently — not exclusively will this form mindfulness of opposing ways of behaving, it will take into consideration better preparation, diminish overpower, and increment your feeling of positive thinking for what's to come. (Cheerfully, one of the 7 Daily Habits of the Whole Life Challenge is Reflection — so this essential step is as of now incorporated into your Challenge insight).

Could it be said that you are Ready to Overcome Resistance?
Change can feel convoluted. Yet, my key important point is this — anticipate obstruction and plan for it.

Protection from change is ordinary. You're probably going to encounter it at some level while attempting to change, paying little mind to how positive your planned change is. Do whatever it takes not to battle obstruction. All things considered, acknowledge it will work out. By perceiving opposition and understanding the reason why it works out, you can zero in your energy on rolling out certain improvements in stick long haul.

Furthermore, by investing a little energy contemplating the possible hindrances, barricades, and obstructions you might experience during the change interaction, you can decrease your degrees of opposition, increment your odds of coming out on top — and beat the opposition.

the most effective method to emergency your assignment list

"Give your very best, with what you have, where you are." — Theodore Roosevelt

Your Outcome: Learn how to manage a blast of approaching things to do and requests on your time.

"Emergency" is a course of arranging, filtering, and choosing what to deal with. You could have found out about specialists "triaging" their approaching patients in crisis settings.

At the point when I previously joined Microsoft, "Emergency" was a typical practice our group used to manage our approaching issues.

It assisted us with arranging our excesses and lines of issues into additional significant containers.

We couldn't simply do everything simultaneously and we were unable to stay aware of our progression of approaching solicitations. Triaging helped us all the more realistically take full advantage of recent memory, energy, and assets we had available right now against our approaching activities.

Emergency in Practice
I've utilized emergency effectively to manage all that from managing email to managing a surge of approaching undertakings to managing maturing over abundance of things to do, both at the individual and the group level.

At the point when I lead a disseminated group, I use email emergencies as an impromptu and lightweight method for getting the group's eyeballs immediately centered around an issue.

I've likewise utilized emergency to clear my email inbox and to keep my email at zero inboxes for quite a long time, and I've shown numerous others, including groups around Microsoft, to do likewise (and we have a great deal of email at Microsoft.)

I tenderly call this methodology, The Zen of Zero Mail.

For things that you want to follow up on, focus on, or get off your plate, "emergency" is a solid course of arranging and choosing carefully.

Email Triage: Do It, Queue It, Schedule It, or Delegate It
You can emergency an approaching thing to do to either make it happen, line it, plan it, or agent it:

Do It - Do it assuming this moment is the opportunity: it's the following best thing for you to do; this moment is the most entrepreneurial opportunity; or it will set you back more agony, time, or work to do it later.

Line It - Queue-it, by adding it to your line on the off chance that it's something you want to finish, however, this present time isn't the ideal open door. A line is just a rundown of things to do.

Plan It - Schedule it by adding it to your schedule if you want a block of time to finish the work. Possibly add things to your schedule if you genuinely need an update or on the other hand assuming that you truly need to close off a piece of time to deal with it. Recollect that assuming you plan it, it will work out, however on the off chance that you don't, it will not. If it's truly significant, set aside a few minutes for it. If it's simply something worth talking about to do "later," and it will not work out, then, at that point, just let it go with ability.

Delegate It - Delegate it assuming something ought to be finished by another person and it's a good idea to do as such, and you have that choice. At the point when you delegate, attempt to match it to someone else's learning an open door or energy. (There's a contrast between designating and unloading.)

3 Steps to Triaging Your Action Items

The following are three stages for triaging your pile of things to do:

Combine your things to do. Managing them in a bunch truly shows the advantage of this methodology, since you can rapidly whack your stack down to measure.

Emergency everything. For everything, figure out what the best game plan is: Do It, Queue It, Schedule It, or Delegate It.

Rehash the interaction. Rehash the cycle until you have a sensible arrangement of activities and you feel that things are properly and perfectly positioned, either in your rundown of activities, your line, your timetable, or off your plate. If you wind up investing a lot of energy triaging, and insufficient time doing, then lay out a timebox or time breaking point to find a steady speed and to know when to stop.

Truly the thing you're doing is making way for your prosperity. By possessing energy for things, and having them on your schedule or in your line, you can zero in on what you have before you with more certainty, lucidity, and conviction, realizing that you're capitalizing on what you have. You can likewise more successfully focus on MUST, SHOULD, and COULD.

Inquiries to Help Guide You
Here are a few inquiries I track down helpful as a designated spot:

What is it that you need to achieve?
Does it matter?
How significant is it?
What's the effect?
What's the following best thing to do?
You can continuously check your activities against the master plan and what you need to achieve: This is only a beginning stage and you'll need to make and test your inquiries to see what works for you.

Assembling It All

We should make a speedy stride back and do an overview of what you've realized such a long way during 30 Days of Getting Results and how this fits in:

You can utilize The Rule of 3 to try not to get overpowered.
You're an incredible writer and you can compose your story forward, each second or one day in turn
You can utilize three stories to drive your day and light up your day by associating with your qualities (Daily Outcomes).
On Mondays, you can utilize three stories to drive your week (Monday Vision).
On Fridays, you can utilize Friday Reflection to praise your successes and make your progress designs.
You can outline what's significant in your life utilizing Hot Spots to make a significant guide.
You can allow things to bog off with ability … no more straws crushing the camel's spirit.
You can make space in your life to restore and re-energize by defining limits and cushions.

You can dump your cerebrum to let loose your brain.

You can focus on more by utilizing MUST, SHOULD, and COULD.

You can feel week long by investing more energy in your assets and less time in your shortcomings.

You can lay out float ways to work on your day and make your schedules grinding-free.

You can examine and be more useful in any situation utilizing efficiency personas.

By adding triaging to your belt, you presently have a basic mental model for managing approaching things to do all the more real.

Coordinated Result is a straightforward framework for significant outcomes that you can use to help you until the end of your life, regardless of what you do. Excellence isn't seriously it's basic or that it's demonstrated ...

It's that every day you get another opportunity at bat - a new beginning. Every day you awaken is one more opportunity to pose the inquiry, "What are three things you need for now?" … Thus you compose your story forward, each day in turn.

The present Assignment
At the point when an approaching thing to do comes your direction, emergency it and choose whether to Do It, Queue It, Schedule It or Delegate It.
Emergency one of your heaps of intentions for whack it down to measure.

A lot To Do? Instructions to Focus Your Attention, Triage Your Tasks, and Regain Your Sanity

When you get up toward the beginning of the day, is your psyche previously working at max speed? You haven't even gotten up, however, your psychological plan for the day shocks your consciousness like a multitude of hornets. Nervousness snatches you by the throat and says, "Hey now, how about we get going . . . there's stuff to do, and you're not kidding."

35

It could have begun hours sooner, denying you rest. (At any point, notice how much more regrettable everything appears to be around midnight?) It establishes the vibe all day long. Rather than having an invigorated outlook on the day, you simply need to snatch a spoon and a container of Ben and Jerry's for breakfast.

It helps me to remember visiting a carnival on the most active day of summer. You pay a lot of cash to go through the day and live it up. However, it's hot - and you're ravenous - and it's packed - and the lines are long - and your children are crying - and it's turbulent. By the day's end, you're more depleted than invigorated.

Not an incredible method for beginning your day.

You probably won't encounter this frequently. Or on the other hand, perhaps it's an everyday event for you.

However, we've all been there - and it doesn't feel better.

Arrangements that Don't Solve Anything
At the point when we're overpowered with activities, it's difficult to tell where to begin. When we pick one thing to work on, all the other things on the rundown begin shouting for our consideration. It's difficult to focus due to the clamor inside our heads.

At the point when that occurs, a large portion of us utilize one of three normal methodologies:

We pick something truly basic and short to do.

It probably won't be vital, however, it gives us a speedy mark (and a dopamine rush). So we're zeroing in on the amount, attempting to traverse whatever the number of things would be prudent so our rundown gets more limited. (Have you at any point achieved something that wasn't on your rundown, and added it so you could verify it?)

We pick something significant yet get occupied when it turns out to be hard.

We have extraordinary aims; yet when we stall out, we browse our email or virtual entertainment. It cheers us up, however, we need to intellectually incline back capable. That is intense because we're advancing toward torment - so the assignment appears to be much more dreadful than it did previously.

Chapter Two: We use the resolution to finish stuff.

It seems like we ought to simply have self-control, so we want to "take care of business." That's an issue since we have a restricted measure of resolution every day. In their book Switch: How to Change Things When Change Is Hard, Chip and Dan Heath found that when we use resolution on one assignment, we have less need for different undertakings. As the day goes on, our determination runs out.

Those techniques could work for some time, however, they're not economical. Why?

Since they disregard how our minds work.

The Science of Paying Attention
It's not difficult to expect that high-performing individuals are simply preferred scholars over low-performing individuals. Their cerebrums simply work unexpectedly, so most of us are ill-fated to lesser things.

Yet, it's false.

Research has shown that our brainpower is shockingly comparable. The vast majority have generally a similar measure of capacity accessible - and it's huge. We can cling to an astonishing measure of data.

Be that as it may, we as a whole have a tiny work area.

That work area is where we concentrate. Assuming there are an excessive number of things in our work area, we lose our capacity to focus.

Consider it a work area in your office. It's intended to be your "work" space, not your "capacity" space. It's where you finish work.

At the point when that work area has heaps all over the place, it's difficult to focus. There are such a large number of things to get our attention when the ongoing undertaking gets hard.

You could say, "Definitely, I have an untidy work area - yet I know precisely where everything is." That's perfect. However, that is regarding your work area as a stockpiling place rather than a work area.

The issue with an untidy work area isn't the messiness; it's the potential for the interruption.

It makes sense to me. I've generally had a muddled work area, encompassed by a chaotic office. I used to have signs that said, "A spotless work area is the indication of a wiped out mind" and "Imaginative personalities are seldom clean."

Be that as it may, it's simply a reason. To the center, I quite often go to an alternate area so I'm not occupied.

Our psychological work area is the same way. It's a little work area to finish something, not to store a lot of other stuff.

What's the arrangement? You want to employ a bouncer.

Why You Need a Bouncer
Dr. Edward Vogel is a scientist at the University of Chicago and is a specialist in consideration.

He says that our brains are astounding, yet they can zero in on a limited quantity of data from your current circumstance at some random time. Many things are seeking that small work area.

His idea: We want to make a bouncer keep the non-significant data off the work area.

A top-of-the-line club recruits a bouncer who remains by the entry. That individual has the list of attendees of VIPs that have been welcomed. Their responsibility is to permit just the welcomed visitors in, and to dismiss every other person - regardless of how boisterous or stubborn or persuasive they may be.

For what reason do we want a psychological bouncer? To keep all that off our work area except what's generally basic at some random time.

Considerably intriguing this:

Superior workers, rather than holding bunches of data as a main priority, hold undeniably less. They're great at taking complex data and focusing on what the most applicable/basic pieces are.

Low entertainers attempt to bring more data than they can oversee at one time.

The thing that matters is the bouncer's viability since it permits us to accomplish complex objectives in the wide range of various interruptions.

Emergency Your Tasks
Where do we get a bouncer? We make one.

A bouncer is made when we become completely clear on our most significant objectives. These incorporate the significant things, yet not pressing - the things that are "strategic" in your work and your own life.

There likewise creator Jim Collins calls BHAGs - "Enormous, Hairy, Audacious Goals." They're the objectives that can change everything in our life assuming we contact them. They're not objectives for the following 5 months; they're objectives that could require a very long time to reach.

At the point when we're sure about our BHAGs, it figures out who's on the "list of people to attend." We give that run down to the bouncer, who then figures out which exercises are important toward those objectives, and which are unessential.

Perhaps you need to begin a business, run a long-distance race, discount a novel or pay your home loan. From where you are at this moment, the objective appears to be far off. In any case, you likewise know that assuming you accomplish that objective, everything would be unique:

When you began your business, you could stop your impasse.
When you run a long-distance race, you'll be more grounded than ever.
When you compose and distribute a novel, you can fill in as a creator.
When you take care of your home loan, you'll have independence from the rat race.
The crucial step is that those objectives aren't pressing, so delaying the subsequent stage until tomorrow is simple. In any case, recollect the expressions of Goethe: Things which make the biggest difference should never be helpless before things that make the least significant difference.

Things which make the biggest difference should never be helpless before things that make the least significant difference.

Take a period today to emergency your plan for the day. What are the main seven assignments that will have the most noteworthy result assuming you did them? Circle them, and cause them the principal things you to do during the day.

Then record your BHAG. What is something that could have a colossal effect on your life assuming you accomplished it? Presently go through your daily agenda and circle each errand that is straightforwardly connected with that major objective.

On the off chance that you track down nothing, conclude what the subsequent stage ought to be that will push you ahead toward accomplishing it. Put it on the list of people to attend as the #1 VIP, and do it first thing in your day.

What will occur? You'll begin your day stimulated because you didn't simply battle your direction through your plan for the day. You made some difference on the things that make the biggest difference.

Chapter Three: step-by-step instructions to designate opportunities to supply

Normally, when you cross one thing off your daily agenda, two more show up. In this manner, the following are 15-time allotment procedures to assist you with staying aware of the timetable. time distribution methods to work on your efficiency
They say that whoever figures out how to dominate time will turn out to be almighty.

On second thought, there is a trace of validity in this since people are equipped for extraordinary things as long as they have the opportunity and willpower to accomplish them.

To help your efficiency, I have arranged for you 15-time usage distribution methods:
-
  - The Pomodoro Technique
  - Task Batching
  - Eating the Frog
  - Brilliant Hours
  - Eisenhower Matrix
  - 80/20 rule
  - Mechanize your errands
  - Plan your day
  - Make plans for the day
  - Focus on assignments
  - Kill interruptions
  - Elon Musk's "time obstructing" technique
  - Track your time (use time following applications)

Characterize MITs (most significant errands)
Don't perform multiple tasks (loss of efficiency)
These tips probably won't show you how to dominate time yet they could carry you nearer to the objective.

How to oversee time?

There is a wide range of time usage systems that you can apply without much of a stretch apply to your everyday exercises to diminish your feelings of anxiety.

Everything relies upon your objectives and self-restraint since you could design well yet you additionally need to adhere to the timetable you made to be useful.

Subsequently, you ought to be reasonable and make feasible timetables.

I understand that you are anxious to handle all that in one day however even machines need some rest in case they overheat.

You should try different things with a variety of strategies, procedures, and frameworks until you figure out which one works the best for you.

1. The Pomodoro Technique
Toggle says that this procedure can be an answer to your concerns on the off chance that you have

seen that your colleagues or representatives get quickly flustered.

You should simply convince them to set the clock.

The strategy conveys your responsibility all the more equally for the day and assists you with maintaining your attention on the errand.

Take your daily agenda
Pick the assignment you need to finish
Set your clock briefly block (otherwise known as one Pomodoro).
Don't perform multiple tasks, and don't intrude on your functioning cycle with little interruptions. Work exclusively on your preferred assignment.
At the point when the time is up, you have procured yourself a 5-minute break.
After 4 patterns of Pomodoros, have some time off - 20-ish minutes.
2. Task Batching

Assuming you are continually performing multiple tasks yet understand that by the day's end you haven't finished a solitary one of your tasks, the undertaking grouping strategy can be the right one for you.

Get your plan for the day and a lot of highlighters and get to work.

time portion methods to work on your efficiency The objective is to find a couple of errands in your rundown that are comparative and should be possible on the double.

With the assistance of various highlighters, you will want to bunch exercises into classes in light of their likenesses.

You may be accustomed to handling dire matters first and this could change the request a little, yet it will make you more useful than previously if you will generally become derailed without any problem.

3. Eating the Frog
Is it true or not that you are battling to finish the really difficult and upsetting jobs? Is it true or not that you love dawdling?

Once more, get your past companion - the plan for the day, and a taste of boldness, and do the most exceedingly terrible errand you see on the rundown.

This method is enlivened by Mark Twain who once said that if a man's work consists of eating a frog, the principal thing he ought to do in the first part of the day is to eat that frog. Perhaps he might have utilized a more charming guide to delineate his message.

At any rate, the thought is that an individual ought to manage the most disagreeable errands of the day. Then, at that point, it just improves.

4. Brilliant hours
It is difficult to remain inspired consistently. An individual is continually impacted by different

conditions, temperaments, sentiments, and considerations.

Accordingly, you shouldn't pass judgment on yourself brutally on the off chance that you are inadequate in concentration or inspiration.

This time usage action is very like the Circadian Rhythm with the sole contrast that you can do it for individual purposes, rather than for attempting to fabricate the ideal group.

Begin a diary where you report your typical business days. Attempt to save it for a week or thereabouts.

Portray how your day is going and when you are feeling the most useful to track down the example. This will assist you with deciding your brilliant hours.

From here on out, you'll know when to take on the more energy-requesting stuff.

5. The Eisenhower Matrix

This time portion procedure is connected with the sensation of bewilderment when you have lots of work and no thought about where to begin.

time portion strategies to work on your efficiency

Snatch a clear piece of paper and separate it into four equivalent quadrants.
At the top, mark the two sections "Pressing" and "Not Urgent".
Name the columns "Significant" and "Not Important".
Drop your undertakings into their assigned classifications.
At the point when you have them generally requested, follow this framework:
Earnest and Important: First to be finished.
Earnest and Not Important: Next in line.
Not Urgent and Important: Create an arrangement for the activity.
Not Urgent and Not Important: Why trouble by any means? Scratch them off.

This is perfect all alone yet could likewise be a supplement to some other prioritization procedure.

6. 80/20 rule

The 80/20 rule, otherwise called the Pareto Principle, is a period portion method that recommends that our day-to-day undertakings are separated into 2 segments - fundamental and minor.

The indispensable undertakings take up 20% of our plan for the day, while the paltry, more basic, assignments are 80%.

It is critical to comprehend this standard since it very well may be applied to everything in our life. Counting dealing with our organizations.

💡 Ace tip

Figure out what are the main undertakings for the afternoon and spotlight your experience on them. This will assist you with being more useful and effective. The 80/20 rule can be applied to all that in your life yet it's particularly useful on the off chance that you maintain a business.

Before you start work, consistently ask yourself, "Is this undertaking in the main 20% of my exercises or the last 80%?"

The standard for this is: to oppose the compulsion to clear up little things first.

7. Mechanize your undertakings
I bet you're tired of managing monotonous manual undertakings that a machine could undoubtedly accomplish for you. All you want is the right programming or a bunch of devices.

The course of robotization could lessen functional expenses, increment unwavering quality, and give you additional time that you can spend on something of more noteworthy significance.

Various stages could offer you the best mechanizing instruments.

You may be asking what could be mechanized.

Advertising, all the more explicitly - web-based entertainment posts.
Managerial errands like booking arrangements and arranging messages.
Money and bookkeeping - overseeing solicitations and working out deals.
8. Plan your day
Assuming that you plan your day ahead of time, you'll be far more coordinated. That is reality.

You could believe that you'll systemize what you are doing over the day or when you awaken, but generally, that is not the situation.

You could awaken and not feel in that frame of mind for doing anything specific, that is the reason you ought to have an unmistakable thought from the other day.

Self-control likewise assumes a tremendous part, since, in such a case that you are maintaining your own business, then, at that point, you don't have a manager to let you know what you MUST do.

You'll need to propel yourself and never pay attention to that internal voice that attempts to convince you that stalling is a decent choice.

9. Make plans for the day
Plans for the day are definitive time portion devices since they provide you with a reasonable thought of what is left for you to finish.

time assignment strategies to work on your efficiency
On the off chance that you don't get every one of the errands on paper or you neglect to refresh your all-around existing show, you could fail to remember something.

A business visionary's day is a rushed one, don't depend on your great memory.

At the point when you put everything in writing, you are likewise ready to think about your assignments and group together some of them.

We should not disregard identity fulfillment when you cross something off the rundown, which can rouse and move you to do one more.

10. Focus on undertakings
I previously referenced the 80/20 rule. It is a delineation of the proportion of immaterial to significant exercises.

To be productive, you ought to focus on and complete significant errands first.

They could take additional time; they may be more challenging to handle. Nonetheless, by the day's end, they will be far more advantageous in contrast with the rest.

If you become accustomed to managing the paltry tasks, you will continuously leave the most squeezing matters for later which is a flat-out no in the expert world.

Likewise, finishing the more unimportant jobs could leave you with an underhanded inclination that your day has been productive, which isn't true.

11. Dispense with interruptions
There is this platitude that we make arrangements so life (or predetermination) could drop them. Consider interruptions as life's little endeavors to lose you on the street.

Obviously, on the off chance that it is something truly significant, you ought to manage it ASAP.

Yet, don't burn through an excess of time focusing on what won't harm you an incredible arrangement or help you an extraordinary arrangement.

Time designation is not an accurate science and you ought to constantly remember that unforeseen things occur and they could postpone you.

Attempt to be ready and whatever occurs, don't lose center around your objectives.

12. Elon Musk's "time obstructing" technique
What time portion procedure does Elon Musk utilize? It's so straightforward but so effective.

Partition your entire day into 5 minutes openings.
Request the undertakings for the afternoon and ponder what amount of time everyone will require.
Allot errands to explicit time allotments in your schedule.
Execute those errands precisely as it is given in your schedule. Try not to drag out, and don't perform multiple tasks.
Once opening = one movement.
This technique will consolidate your daily agenda with your schedule and will assist you with keeping away from tarrying.

13. Track your time

At the point when you track your time, you know what amount of time a particular errand requires for you. This could help you hugely when you plan your following day.

time designation procedures to work on your efficiency

You'll have an unmistakable thought regardless of whether an errand is tedious and you'll have the option to structure better timetables and fulfill time constraints.

You'll likewise be aware of how much time is spent on insignificant exercises and you'll either diminish it or continue toward the following thing.

It'll be simpler for you to see that you're stalling out.

14. Characterize MITs

As I have rehashed a couple of times in this article, any business visionary should have the option to recognize the Most Important Tasks and the ones that could stand by a little.

Yet, how would you do that?

What is the most significant among them all?

Whatever might influence your pay ought to be viewed as basic and ought to be managed ASAP.

It doesn't make any difference whether it has a negative or a constructive outcome, do that first!

Typically, you ought to have a couple of squeezing matters of this sort each day. They will generally be more convoluted and tedious, consequently, you ought to never allow them to stack up!

15. Don't perform various tasks

Performing multiple tasks is the main adversary of time designation methods in light of multiple factors.

You get quickly flustered.
You begin doing various things simultaneously and they end up uncompleted.
You don't follow a reasonable arrangement and you could get befuddled.
Being overpowered by responsibility is likewise a key disadvantage.
Regardless of whether you figure out how to finish everything, the nature of execution will not be essentially as great as it would be if you had zeroed in on each thing in turn.
Generally, I profoundly exhort you against taking up this action regardless of how brief a period you are left with.

It's smarter to apologize, make sense of and do it appropriately with a postponement, rather than making a mess up out of the errand.

Consolidate different time assignment methods to defeat your day

I trust that we've figured out how to give you the best manual for time usage exercises and that you'll have the option to go into the day more certainly than any time in recent memory.

Remember that you can involve different time portion techniques for various circumstances and you can likewise join a couple of them to be pretty much as productive as could be expected.

Try, evaluate various things, and see what has exactly the intended effect for you.

All things considered, a genuine time ace has many stunts at its disposal.

PS. Remember old fashioned time usage worksheets. An hour of arranging saves you long periods of doing.

One more move toward the same Direction

10 hints to oversee time and assignments

1. Ponder your ongoing way to deal with overseeing time and assignments
2. Distinguish requests on your time
3. Focus on
4. Separate undertakings
5. Augment efficiency
6. Use arranging devices
7. Limit tarrying
8. Keep up with inspiration
9. Tell others your plan
10. Foster a standard report design

Related Assets

Individuals start college with currently bustling lives with significant responsibilities or needs notwithstanding study. Effectively dealing with your needs and responsibilities requires a coordinated way to deal with both times and undertaking the executives.

1. Ponder your ongoing way to deal with overseeing time and assignments

Ponder how you commonly oversee time in your regular daily existence. Monitoring your propensities (both great and terrible), inclinations, qualities, and shortcomings assists you with distinguishing techniques to capitalize on your time and remain persuaded.

To start with, contemplate your ongoing methodology. Ask yourself:

Do I for the most part design my time?
Do I get a kick out of the chance to be on time and have things done on time?
Do I find it generally simple to shuffle contending assignments?
Am I ready to focus on errands?
Do I utilize devices to design my time?
If you addressed yes for the greater part of these, you may as of now be a remarkable time chief! This asset will in any case give you a few new tips and methodologies. Assuming you addressed no for the greater part of these, that is OK, you're being straightforward with yourself.

You will profit from the tips and methodologies in this asset.

Get some information about your ongoing methodology. Do you think that it is unpleasant, inspiring, or sufficient? Are there any angles you might want to move along?

Remember these reflections as you consider how you could execute the accompanying procedures.

2. Distinguish requests on your time
The best understudies are the individuals who have healthy lifestyles. That implies they make time every week for exercises like research and chipping away at tasks, as well as paid work, caring obligations, dozing, working out, appreciating leisure activities, and investing energy with loved ones.

Begin by making a rundown of all of your:

College responsibilities: staying aware of the week-by-week readings and content, concentrating on time, appraisals, conversation gatherings, online courses, and so on.

3. Focus on

Whenever you've distinguished the requests on your time, conclude what is adaptable and what isn't. Take a stab at sorting errands arranged by significance and worth utilizing a straight line like the one underneath.

Things that are of high significance and worth truly ought to be remembered for your preparation - outline these on the left half of the line. Low significance and low assignments go on the right.

For example, An evaluation task worth 60% of the subject imprint due in three weeks is high worth and significant - this is important. Re-requesting the books on your shelf might give you fulfillment however is low significance, low worth, and isn't vital.

Focusing on undertakings arranged by significance or worth. The errands that are named high significance are on the left, and they go all together towards the right side. At the super left there is a significant task worth half, then, at that point, perusing for the following instructional exercise, a minor evaluation task worth 5%, then, at that point, a virtual entertainment feed lastly at the super right re-requesting your shelf.

Exercises of significance ought to be outlined by a semester organizer.

4. Separate assignments
It can now and again be hard to get everything rolling on bigger errands as how much work is required can appear to be overpowering. To make it more reasonable, have a go at separating errands into more modest, more feasible objectives.

5. Boost efficiency

It's essential to utilize your time concentrating as actually and effectively as could be expected.

Contemplate:

Your best pinnacle focus times: morning, evening, or night.
The blocks of time you have accessible: plan these inside your best fixation times considering your family and home climate.
Planning short, serious review meetings instead of long, long-distance race ones: short, escalated times of study implies you can keep up both your focus and nature of work. Plan these for 1-2 hours with breaks between them. E.g.:
Study

Differing your review exercises: at whatever point conceivable pick dynamic learning techniques, and accomplish something with the materials you're considering, for example, attempt re-shaping your notes into a flowchart or mind map (dynamic procedure), as opposed to simply re-understanding them (latent).

Your learning inclinations: find how you like to study and make those circumstances for yourself.

6. Use arranging devices

Organizers assist you with delineating your time and undertakings outwardly. Both on the web and paper renditions are powerful - consider which would turn out best for you.

A semester organizer is perfect for providing you with an outline of the whole semester, permitting you to see when your bustling periods for evaluation will happen so you can fan out the responsibility, rather than doing everything simultaneously. Ensure you input task accommodation dates here.

A week-after-week organizer (DOC 83.0 KB) assists you with outlining your week-after-week responsibilities (class, review, and individual), considering top fixation times, and choosing when to get things done.

Plans for the day are an incredible approach to keeping on top of your everyday undertakings. These can be short speck point arrangements of things you want to do on a given day. Tick them off as you finish them.

Take a stab at utilizing the task organizer (DOC 49.5 KB) to separate your tasks into stages and to decide the course of events you want to follow to finish the work by the set cutoff time effectively.

7. Limit hesitation

Frequently, the most horrendously terrible part about having a great deal to do isn't the actual work but the concern related to it. Assuming you need to fight to stall, it is possible that you have not worked out an approach to dealing with an errand.

Hesitation can be your approach to saying, "I don't have the foggiest idea how to begin". It may not be lethargy - it very well may be more about focus.

Hostile to lingering techniques

Perceive while you're lingering (additional work area cleaning, playing 'one more game on your telephone).

Distinguish why you're tarrying: you may not completely grasp the errand; you might not have a cycle for working.

Separate the errand into reasonable lumps: split it up into more modest pieces, for example, dissect the errand, conceptualize thoughts, discover a few readings, make notes, compose a draft, alter, and submit.

Begin with additional reasonable exercises: for example, perusing a short article before a more extended one.

Set more limited, reachable times. For example, Let yourself know you'll chip away at something for 20 minutes and check whether you can continue onward.

Plan standard short review blocks of 1-2 hours (structure propensities) with the concentrate on targets - this provides you guidance and cutoff points.

Look for help when you want it: on the off chance that you don't figure out the undertaking, converse with somebody.

Be sensible in your objectives: "In the time I have I want to finish …."

Measure and commend your advancement: have quantifiable targets (read one article, compose 200 words) - give yourself little compensation for accomplishing them.

8. Keep up with inspiration

Numerous understudies experience issues remaining persuaded sooner or later during their examinations and their time and assignment the executives vacillate alongside it. Here and there this is because of indifference, while at different times it might connect with trouble. Absence of inspiration and delaying are frequently interrelated: when you lose inspiration, you likewise end up hindered by absolutely everything that could remove you from the study.

You will not be similarly keen on all that you concentrate on so you want to track down ways of inspiring yourself to concentrate on the things you're not enthusiastic about.

Track down a point in the subject
Attempt to interface what you are realizing with certifiable circumstances. Sort out why the ideas or abilities are applicable or helpful for your future vocation. If you continue in the improvement of this ability, will it give you an edge for future business? Have a go at watching video cuts on the point - alternate points of view on it might give you a new way to deal with it.

Associate with others
One of the most incredible ways of concentrating successfully and remaining inspired at college is fully backed by your friends. You might track down the substance troublesome multi-week yet another person might comprehend it well and in different weeks the inverse may be valid. It merits requiring investment to associate with cohorts in web-based conversation gatherings or by

shaping review gatherings, on the off chance that you can meet.

Change your strategies
An absence of inspiration can frequently come from doing things in a similar redundant way. Take a stab at shaking things up, for example, different review strategies or areas.

9. Tell others your schedule
Overseeing and concentrating on undertakings must be accomplished according to the remainder of your life, and that implies simply deciding, preparing, and speaking with individuals in your day-to-day existence.

Once in a while this implies saying "no" to companions, to family, or to extra time at work: it's tied in with focusing on.

Examine your review schedule with loved ones, put the plan on the cooler or give them a duplicate. This can set them mindful of the expectations in your day-to-day existence and assist them with grasping your needs.

10. Foster an ordinary report design
Laying out a customary example of work can assist with getting you into a daily schedule. This permits you to feel more in charge (which ought to assist with lingering), squeeze all expected errands into the time accessible, and expand your time use. An approach to beating tarrying issues is the foundation of everyday practice.

At long last
Make sure to keep balance in your life. Focus on what's essential to you, or more all be practical in the objectives you set, and make partitions: when you are considering, study, when you are unwinding - do that, unwind!

Chapter Four: the most effective method to execute your arrangement

Organizations frequently depend on project chiefs to create and execute plans to guarantee their activities are effective. A top-notch plan can guarantee vital arrangement, give clear concentration and targets, increment quality, decline costs, and further develop efficiency. If you deal with a group or tasks, you might be keen on figuring out how to lead a successful arrangement. In this article, we talk about why arranging is significant, share key stages to execute a viable arrangement, and give tips to assist you with arranging your next project effectively.

Having an arrangement is significant because it can give you rules and activity moves toward completing a task. Effective venture chiefs frequently intend to discuss their objectives with their group, partners, clients, supporters, and others engaged with the undertaking. Executing an advanced arrangement can assist you with remaining coordinated, keeping tabs on your development, and guaranteeing a venture's general achievement.

It can likewise give you a reference to return to toward the finish of the task, which can assist you with figuring out what was fruitful and where there is an opportunity to get better. This might assist you with making considerably more fruitful plans from now on.

Step-by-step instructions to execute a successful arrangement
Here are a few stages you can follow to help you create and execute a viable arrangement for your next project:

1. Accumulate data

Before you can start fostering a fruitful arrangement, you want to ensure you have all the data essential. Plan a gathering with clients, partners, or other colleagues to decide the full extent of the undertaking. A few inquiries you could pose include:

What are the critical expectations for this undertaking?
What do you think about a fruitful profit from the venture?
Are there any key achievements we ought to know about?
When should this extension be finished?
What correspondence channels does your client like?
What is the main region of the undertaking we ought to zero in on?
What is the spending plan for this task?
What issue does this extend to expect to settle?
Take intensive notes all through your conversation so you can reference them later on when you begin to foster your arrangement.

These notes can likewise be useful to impart to other colleagues to guarantee everybody is adjusted and pursuing accomplishing similar goals.

2. Recognize secret weapons
Whenever you have laid out the extent of the undertaking, consider the secret weapons you want to finish it. These assets can change from one undertaking to another, however frequently incorporate natural substances, gear, programming, staff, and sellers. You can make a rundown to assist you with monitoring these assets or utilize an undertaking the board programming instrument to assist you with remaining coordinated. Utilize a web crawler to investigate different tasks on the board programming instruments and pick the one that turns out best for you.

Whenever you have made your rundown of essential assets, you might start to distinguish where you can source them from. Consider including a reinforcement choice for every asset to guarantee you are good to go. By finding the opportunity to break down what assets your group needs to finish this venture, you can assist with keeping the undertaking on time and improve the probability of its general achievement.

3. Foster SMART objectives

The following stage is to foster clear and noteworthy objectives to assist your group with finishing the venture. Utilizing the SMART objective strategy can assist you with figuring out which targets are the most critical to the task's general achievement. Savvy objectives will be goals that are explicit, quantifiable, reachable, important, and time-sensitive. You can make SMART objectives by zeroing in on every single one of these areas:

Explicit: Use the data you assembled from your client, partners, or group to make objectives with explicit cutoff times and key achievements. Utilize straightforward language to explain what

targets your group needs to accomplish so they can undoubtedly decide if they are effective.
Quantifiable: Identify how you intend to quantify the task's advancement and achievement. You could decide to quantify the number of deals your group creates, the number of things they produce, or the time it takes to accomplish significant achievements. Ensure the metric you pick can be effortlessly followed so you can decide the general outcome of the task.
Attainable: Ensure that the objectives you set are reasonable. Inquire as to whether you can accomplish your objectives with the assets, colleagues, and spending plan you have. If essential, consider making changes in accordance to put your group in a good position.
Significant: Determine how significant the objectives you have set are to the general progress of the task. This can assist you with focusing on your objectives and give your group clear rules.
Time-sensitive: Identify a reasonable course of events for when undertakings should be finished by, when key achievements should be

accomplished and when the venture should be done. This can assist you with keeping your group on the target and screening the venture's general advancement to guarantee your group finishes it on time.

4. Make the system
Whenever you have distinguished SMART objectives, consider how you can move toward the undertaking by separating these objectives into more modest errands. Make a structure that distinguishes each step of the undertaking and when it should be finished by. Project chiefs use systems to furnish their group with rules, layout essential strategies, and guarantee a typical language is utilized for correspondence across the whole group.

Fostering an undertaking structure can likewise assist you to share best practices with your group and assist clients with figuring out the interaction. You can investigate different undertakings of the executives' authoritative designs and pick the one that turns out best for you.

Try not to get yourself in a position for disappointment while astonishing elective prospects are hanging tight for you.

The most effective method to adhere to an arrangement
Ensure your objectives fit inside the terrific plan of your last assumptions.

Whether you're discussing where you need to carry on with your life or what kind of business you need to run, ensuring things integrate is critical.

Envision somebody anticipating a method for beginning a golf ball business while the ultimate objective is to possess a frozen yogurt shop.

Ensuring things are pertinent to each other is a significant stage.

Moreover, when you make arrangements, to build your possibilities by adhering to them, give yourself practical periods.

While it may very well be ideal to imagine that you can turn into a mogul in seven days, the likelihood of that occurrence is low.

Ensure you're defining reachable objectives inside unambiguous periods with the goal that you can give yourself something to pursue and see the improvement as it's being made.

Chapter Five: How Do I Create a Plan And Stick To It

Whenever you've sorted out what your fundamental arrangement is, it's critical to perceive how much time you need to accomplish it.

This is an unbelievably significant stage for slackers.

Perhaps of the most well-known issues, individuals wind up managing and accepting they have considerably more time than they do.

They then, at that point, think of themselves as either behind schedule or having difficult issues.

Accomplish Your Goals

By working in reverse from the set arrangement and putting more modest put forth objectives en route, you can assist with keeping things coordinated and come to the endpoint without issues.

Ensure you give yourself sufficient opportunity and begin working in reverse.

Likewise, consider every one of the more modest advances that will be important to bring the way.

Regardless of how huge of an ultimate objective you have, you can separate it into something more sensible over the long run, making things substantially more conceivable.

Understanding what needs to have occurred for you to arrive at your last objectives, will propel you to accomplish your objectives

Sort Out What You Need
Methodologies for Sticking to Your Goals

Ensuring you have all that you want to effectively accomplish your assumptions is the way to having an arrangement and adhering to it.

Make a thoroughly examined rundown of all that you could try to understand your arrangements. Arrange to get what you want to execute your arrangement.

All that you do from here on out ought to be finished because of productivity.

Like that, you'll be ensured to arrive at your assumptions well before you at any point would have thought.

For instance, If you bring an arrangement to the table for advancements or deals, ensure you have the perfect proportion of items accessible.

Use Lists
Instructions to adhere to objectives

On the off chance that you'd like an obvious sign towards arriving at your objectives, format records with a more modest focus you can check off or feature.

Not exclusively will this be very fulfilling intellectually, however it will assist you with monitoring what has previously been dealt with and what actually should be finished?

These rundowns are an incredible instrument for generally speaking preparation and everyday preparation.

By keeping them up on a wall or back of an entryway, you'll furnish yourself with a consistent sign of what you want to finish.

Take a stab at giving your rundown a particular timetable, for example, "Monday's List" or "Week after week List".

This assists you with giving a particular time in which you can complete each responsibility on that rundown.

step-by-step instructions to adhere to an objective

Without making some particular memories outlined as a primary concern, it's excessively simple for things to move away from you.

Along these lines, keeping things clear like this will cause your ultimate objectives to show up significantly more sensible.

So ensure you take full benefit by making them something you love returning to frequently.

Make Yourself Accountable
Stick to objectives
At the point when the main individual that can cause you to understand your arrangement is yourself, things can frequently get set to the side

as you suspect "I'll do it tomorrow," or "I'll begin one week from now."

All things considered, have a dear companion or relative consider you responsible for anything that you're doing.

Like that, you will feel an awareness of others' expectations and earnestness concerning keeping yourself on target.

Make them completely mindful of what needs to end up arriving at your definitive objectives, and have them be as firm and requesting of you as could be expected.

Adhering to objectives
Frequently enough, simply the possibility of another person monitoring what you want to finish can be all that anyone could need of inspiration.

If you don't have a companion or relative you trust, there are many hierarchical or persuasive gatherings that meet occasionally where you can share your objectives.

Regardless of whether the main steady individual there is the mentor, having somebody who understands what you want to do and who will push you to make it happen can improve things greatly over the long haul.

Embrace Cheat Days
Adhering to your objectives
Whether you're anticipating pizza night or can hardly hold on to giving yourself a little small-scale excursion from your business, enjoying reprieves is a fundamental piece of any fruitful arrangement.

Remaining driven and rapidly arriving at your objectives is a certain something, be that as it may, you shouldn't turn out to be excessively worn out to continue.

By giving yourself a periodic rest day, you'll be a lot better intellectually.

You'll likewise be significantly more prone to partake in your prosperity when you, at last, arrive at it.

These days can be totally helpful.

They will give you a truly necessary jolt of energy to go out there and execute your arrangements.

Give yourself enough rest so you feel rejuvenated and prepared to arrive at your definitive objectives quickly.

Make It All Thoughtless
Carrying out objectives
By transforming specific more modest assignments into careless propensities, you'll be significantly more prone to accomplish your assumptions well before you at any point anticipated.

Having to continually remind yourself to finish specific undertakings and driving yourself right into it can be testing and frequently enough to make you need to abandon your arrangement.

Cause-specific parts of this work neglectful propensities and you'll be en route to progress pretty quickly.

Try not to transform your objectives into a bonus that you're attempting to accomplish.

See making an arrangement and adhere to it as part of your everyday life.

This is fundamental so they never again feel like difficult work each time you start.

Assuming you're to call clients toward the finish of each drawn-out day, make these more modest assignment propensities.

This, thus, will assist you with keeping things more reasonable for you.

Encircle Yourself With The Right People
Step-by-step instructions to adhere to objectives
At the point when you have the right sort of individuals working with you, you effectively make arrangements and stick to them.

The ideal arrangement of representatives can emphatically affect the general outcome of your business.

Making them mindful of your arrangements makes them more able to work with you towards accomplishing them.

Ensure you don't allow yourself to surrender to disappointment by having gloomy individuals around you.

Encircle yourself with inspiration and drive, and you'll have it simply making arrangements and adhering to them.

Follow Your Goals

Having quality staff working with you can be the most ideal way to assist yourself with adhering to your arrangements.

These people will move you and give you the inspiration you want to continue to go each day.

They will make it workable for you to remain fixed on your arrangements and take out each bad attitude.

By making them a piece of your arrangement, you make a group that will battle close by you to vanquish hindrances.

Consequently, provide yourself with the endowment of that sort of help for when you want it most.

Look How Far You've Come
The most effective method to adhere to your objectives

Something you can do while attempting to adhere to an arrangement is to glance back at how far you've come.

Time after time, the progressions you cause become so natural that you fail to remember they weren't in every case part of what your identity is.

By making a stride back and isolating yourself, you'll have the option to see ways you've made sensational contrasts.

At the point when you feel like you're wasting time, ensure you remember all that you've proactively achieved in your arrangement.

Pursuing objectives

By perceiving the achievement you've previously had, you'll be considerably more prone to take a stab at much more achievement.

Try not to allow yourself to get worn out by your arrangement without permitting yourself to feel the award.

Everybody needs a congratulatory gesture occasionally as a commendation for an expert piece of handiwork.

Consequently, make sure to give yourself enough credit so you feel an obligation as well as a longing to continue onward.

Plan for Success
Accomplish Goals

As opposed to getting ready for the most terrible, what you ought to do is set yourself up for something good.

By making arrangements in snapshots of unadulterated energy, you'll be substantially more liable to take a stab at greater objectives.

This will try and assist you with staying in your arrangements and move you quickly towards your ultimate objective.

On the off chance that you're not just staying on track you've spread out, yet attempting to overextend it, you'll assist with transforming your ultimate objective into a genuine example of overcoming adversity before your own eyes.

You ought to give yourself the inspiration you want by letting yourself know that these things will all occur for you.

Have faith in Yourself
Staying with something

All in all, you've spread out your arrangement and you've set up how you plan to adhere to it — what's left?

Have total and complete confidence in yourself to accomplish all that you've arranged.

Truly when you have confidence in yourself and your capacities, you'll set yourself in a situation for progress.

A negative disposition can emphatically affect how much exertion you at last put into understanding your arrangements.

If you as of now feel like you will come up short, what's the point?

By keeping yourself cheerful, realizing that you'll have the option to accomplish anything you set your attention to.

You'll understand your arrangements sometime before you know it.

With regards to making an arrangement, nothing is a higher priority than standing firm.

The most effective method to stay with something

Most times, entrepreneurs surrender their fantasies well before they even get the opportunity to fall flat at them.

By making a thoroughly examined plan and tracking down ways of keeping yourself propelled to stay with it, you'll have the option to move consistently forward and take a stab at progress day to day.

These arranging tips and deceives will assist you with remaining fixed on what's significant.

It will likewise permit you to take serious steps towards your ultimate objective at each open door.

Inspiration and genuine assurance are critical to giving yourself the drive you want to accomplish all that you've at any point arranged.

By removing specific negative behavior patterns from your everyday life and supplanting them with genuine difficult work, you'll begin to get results that you never envisioned conceivably.

Ensure you remember these tips and deceives so you can be headed to progress in the blink of an eye by any means.

Chapter Six: instructions to quit diverting yourself

The most useful individuals on the planet finish each thing in turn.

We've all been there. Indeed, even with good motives to keep focused, we find ourselves looking at virtual entertainment when we ought to be chipping away at a task. We can't resist the urge to snatch our mobile phone the second we hear a notice. And afterward, there's an email! If we aren't checking it like clockwork, we stress we could miss something significant.

Interruptions can appear to be difficult to keep away from. Measurements show that interruptions cause a gigantic misfortune in efficiency. The regular administrator is intruded on like clockwork, and workers by and large invest 28% of their energy managing superfluous interferences and attempting to refocus.

All in all, how might you assume back command over your time and consideration? The following are seven demonstrated procedures for defeating interruptions and recovering your concentration.

1. Put yourself in interruption-free mode.
Start building propensities that assist you with taking out interruptions and keeping on track. Begin by establishing a climate where you're less enticed to get engrossed with some different options from what you're chipping away at. This is generally difficult to do. As far as one might be concerned, a large number of us depend on a PC to take care of our responsibilities, yet we likewise find our greatest interruptions empowered by the utilization of a PC on the web. On the off chance that you continually end up meandering over to video or shopping sites, take a stab at utilizing a site blocker application.

Work to make propensities that sign to yourself and everyone around you that you're in interruption-free mode. Close the way to your office. Put on surrounding sound-blocking earphones. Switch off your telephone or put it on quietly and move it away from you (so you can only with significant effort get it). If you work in an open office, you might find it supportive to move to a calmer area. Investigations have discovered that interruptions happen 64% all the more frequently in an open office, and we're intruded on by others all the more frequently in that climate too.

Eliminate however many reasons and interruptions as you can so you can carry your undivided focus to each undertaking in turn - - no performing various tasks.

2. Set three fundamental goals consistently. An extensive rundown of activities can feel impossible and leave us feeling overpowered. We're prepared to surrender before we start, and

that is the point at which it turns out to be not difficult to yield to interruptions. You can balance this by giving yourself 3 targets to achieve consistently. Keep in touch with them on a sticky note and post it where you can see it each time you gaze upward from your work.

By restricting the number of day-to-day objectives, you'll have characterized what you want to chip away at. You'll work with the more prominent goal on those assignments and your brain will be less adept to wander.

Ask yourself each day: What are the three most significant things to achieve today? Some other errands ought to be placed on a different plan for the day. You can start to handle those less-significant assignments whenever you've achieved the initial 3 objectives.

3. Give yourself a more limited time.
More hours worked doesn't mean you fundamentally get more things achieved. That's what Parkinson's regulation says "work will, in

general, grow to occupy the time we have accessible for its finish." And truly, we for the most part occupy any time staying with interruptions. This is because our psyche is wired to monitor energy whenever the situation allows. If we don't need to follow through with something, there's a decent opportunity we will not make it happen. All things considered, we'll permit ourselves to get sucked into a YouTube video or a game application on our telephone.

Then again, when we're facing a cutoff time, we unexpectedly foster an exacting concentration and keep away from interruptions no matter what. At the point when you realize you need to finish something, you'll sort out a method for making it happen.

To take out interruptions, give yourself a more limited time to complete your work. This resembles giving yourself a fake cutoff time, yet upheld with something that considers you responsible. Tell your chief or client that you'll provide them with a draft of an undertaking before the day's over. Find a responsible accomplice who will hold you to your objective time. Anyway, you make it happen, setting a hard cutoff time will assist you with keeping away from interruptions and amp up your efficiency.

4. Screen your psyche meandering.
We spend almost 50% of our waking time pondering some different options from what we should do, as per one Harvard study. We are progressing automatically, and our psyche is meandering, to a limited extent to keep away from the work of zeroing in on something. The way to uplift efficiency is to see when your psyche is occupied and welcome your consideration back on task.

This implies focusing on your viewpoints and perceiving when your brain begins floating. This permits you to oversee what you center around and divert your contemplations when you goof. Rather than permitting yourself to continue to wander over to virtual entertainment to look at your newsfeed, you effectively put the brakes on this interruption.

Focus on what interruptions are especially difficult to keep away from, so you can get them sooner. At the point when you feel a craving to yield to an interruption, slowly inhale and intentionally decide not to respond to it. Whenever you've yielded and permitted yourself to zero in on something different, such as understanding messages, it's harder to refocus and take your consideration back to the job that needs to be done.

To put it, be aware of your viewpoints, rather than permitting yourself to skip among assignments and interrupt.

5. Train your cerebrum by making a game out of it.
Your psyche resembles a muscle. To utilize it successfully, you want to develop it. We want to prepare our minds to keep on track by slowly

dealing with our fixation. This will reinforce our capacity to concentrate for longer timeframes.

An extraordinary method for starting doing this is through the "Pomodoro Method," in which you set a clock and are centered around an errand for a while, like 45 minutes in a row. Then permit yourself a 15-minute break.

If 45 minutes is a stretch, begin with something more reasonable, like 25 minutes, and afterward offer yourself a five-minute reprieve. The thought is to make a round of it - - challenge yourself to work tenaciously on your errand until the clock rings. Then permit yourself to glut on anything interruption you need, however just for an allocated time frame.

After the break, it has returned to work again until the clock rings. You'll be astonished by the amount you can finish utilizing this strategy!

6. Take on testing work.

Assuming you're experiencing difficulty centering and are constantly occupied, it is possible that your work isn't connecting with you completely. You could feel like you're buckling down the entire day, yet it may be the case that your psyche is battling fatigue and hoping to occupy the time with something seriously fascinating.

Complex errands request a greater amount of our functioning memory and consideration, meaning we have less intellectual ability staying to meander to the closest invigorating interruption. We're probably going to go into a condition of all-out work submersion when our capacities are tested. We get exhausted when our abilities incredibly surpass the requests of our work - -, for example, when we do a careless information section for a few hours.

Evaluate the degree of inefficient busywork you're doing. Might it be said that you are struggling with becoming part of the venture? This could show that you can take on additional difficult undertakings. At the point when we take on more intricate work that pushes our expertise and scholarly cutoff points, we can become consumed and hyper-zeroed in on the errand. Our psyches are wired to zero in on anything novel, pleasurable or compromising. What's more, handling these undertakings provides us with pride.

We have no such feeling of achievement with an undertaking we consider humble.

7. Break the pattern of pressure and interruption. Stress can likewise assume a significant part in our failure to concentrate or defeat interruptions. Time and again, we wind up attempting to work while feeling overpowered. This leaves us fatigued and depleted, quickly drawn off track and incapable of center. Assuming you're quickly drawn off track, it can show that you're under raised pressure.

There's even a name for it: "quickly drawn off track uneasiness." Symptoms include:

You experience issues concentrating and your psyche continually floats from what you were zeroing in on.
You have more trouble shaping considerations and remaining focused than ordinary.
Your reasoning feels tangled and debilitated.
You feel your momentary memory isn't quite so great as it ordinarily is.
Managing your pressure will assist you with recapturing your concentration and beat interruptions all the more without any problem. You should track down ways of quieting your psyche and loosening up your body to decrease the body's pressure reaction. Ensure you get sufficient rest. Work on breathing activities and track down ways of containing your uneasiness.

Chapter Seven: stop outer interruptions

Figure out How To Avoid Distraction In A World That Is Full Of It

Interruption is a scourge of present-day life. Between our phones and PC screens, also our children and collaborators, our consideration is continually being redirected. It can become challenging to zero in on any one assignment — or any one individual — for extremely lengthy.

Regardless, the world is turning into a seriously diverting spot. Innovation is turning out to be more inescapable and convincing. Be that as it may, trusting tech organizations significantly alter their methodologies and your supervisor at last figures out how to regard your time might take more time than you're willing to stand by. Better to prepare yourself to oversee interruption with systems you can execute immediately. After all, although interruptions aren't your shortcoming, overseeing them is your obligation.

In this section, I talk about why interruptions are so unsafe, where they begin, and key methods that will assist you with at long last defeating interruptions for good. This guide is a concise presentation of how you can become indestructible.

Here is a layout of the thing that's coming down the road:

What is an interruption and for what reason is it unsafe?
What is something contrary to interruption?
What causes interruption?
Four techniques for becoming distractable
Ace inward triggers.
Set aside a few minutes for footing.
Hack back outside triggers.
Forestall interruption with agreements.
Help other people keep away from interruption

1. What is an interruption and for what reason is it hurtful?

Interruption is "the most common way of interfering with consideration" and "a boost or errand that distracts from the undertaking of essential interest."1 at the end of the day, interruptions draw us from what we need to do, whether it's to achieve an undertaking at home or work, appreciate time with a friend or family member, or work on something for ourselves.

On the off chance that interruption turns into a propensity, we can't support the center expected for imagination in our expert and individual lives. More terrible, assuming that we are continually pulled away from loved ones by interruptions, we pass up developing the connections we want for our mental prosperity.

So, an interruption is any activity that pulls us from what we truly need to do.

Do you perceive any of these undesirable interruptions?

Taking a gander at notices that spring up on your telephone — in any event, during discussions with family, companions, or partners
Hindering-centered work to browse email
Talking with collaborators who swing by your work area when you planned to accomplish centered work
Looking at your virtual entertainment takes care of when you intended to peruse a book
Allow me to add to these interruption models with one from my own life.

One day my little girl — my lone kid — and I were messing around together in an action book intended to bring daddies and little girls closer together. We asked each other the question, "If you could have any superpower, what might it be?"

I want to let you know my girl's response, yet I can't because I wasn't there.

"Daddy?" she questioned.

"Simply a second," I snorted, "I want to answer a certain something." My eyes were stuck to my telephone, my fingers tapping ceaselessly.

When I looked into it, she was no more.

I had quite recently blown an extraordinary second with my girl since I had permitted something on my telephone to divert me.

All alone, that episode is nothing to joke about. Notwithstanding, the scene rehashed the same thing a few times. If I planned to carry on with the sort of life I needed, I realized I needed to change, and chances are, so do you.

Interruptions aren't your shortcoming, however, overseeing them is your obligation.

2. What is something contrary to interruption?

If you would rather not be occupied, probably you need its inverse. In any case, assuming you search "interruption antonym," you will see that "interruption" doesn't have a careful inverse. Merriam-Webster truly does propose a few "close to antonyms" like confirmation, sureness, certainty, and conviction.2 That doesn't help when you want to create some distance from interruption — toward what? I propose embracing the expression "footing" as something contrary to interruption.

Foothold is any activity that moves us towards what we truly care about.

Any activity, like chipping away at a major task, getting sufficient rest or actual activity, eating quality food, finding the opportunity to ponder or supplicate, or investing energy with friends and family, is the type of footing. Foothold is any activity you do with purpose. It's doing what you say you will do.

3. What causes interruption?

All human ways of behaving are signaled by one or the other outside or inward triggers.

Outer triggers are prompts from our current circumstances that guide us next. These are the dings and pings that expeditious us to browse our email, answer a text, or take a gander at a news alert. Contest for our consideration can emerge from an individual too, for example, a break from a collaborator when we are busy accomplishing centered work. Indeed, even an article can be an outside trigger: your TV appears to encourage you to turn it on by its simple presence.

Inner triggers are signs from inside us. At the point when we're eager, we are signaled to grab a bite; when we feel a chill, we put on a sweater. At the point when we're focused on or desolate, we could call a companion for help. Inside triggers are pessimistic sentiments.

Since all conduct is incited by one or the other outside or inside triggers, then, at that point, both the activities we expect to do (foothold) as well as those that become sidetracked (interruption), start from a similar source.

Interruption is an unfortunate getaway from terrible sentiments.

4. Four systems for becoming distractable
On the off chance that you are prepared to reclaim your life from unremitting interruptions, you want to follow four moves toward becoming distractable:

Ace inward triggers.
Set aside a few minutes for a foothold.
Hack back outer triggers.
Forestall interruption with settlements.
Like what you're pursuing? This article draws on my book Indistractable: How to Control Your Attention and Choose Your Life. You can buy it here and buy into my bulletin to get more incredible articles.

A. Ace inside triggers.

To conquer interruptions, you want to comprehend what drives your ways of behaving — what prompts you to take a gander at your telephone or read another email urgently.

The underlying driver of the human way of behaving is the craving to get away from distress. In any event, when we assume we are looking for delight, we're determined by the longing to liberate ourselves from the aggravation of needing.

In all actuality, we abuse computer games, online entertainment, and our PDAs for the joy they give, but since they free us from mental distress.

Interruption, then, is an unfortunate getaway from terrible feelings. Once you can perceive the job inside triggers like weariness, depression, weakness, exhaustion, and vulnerability play in your life, you can choose how to answer in a better way. You have no control over how you feel, yet you can figure out how to control how you respond to how you feel.

To begin, you can change your opinion on those awful sentiments that can prompt interruption.

Concentrates on demonstrating the way that not surrendering to a desire can misfire. Opposing a hankering or drive can set off rumination and cause the longing to develop stronger.3 When you at last surrender, letting that strain free from needing expands the prize, conceivably making an unfortunate behavior pattern. Fortunately, there are more brilliant ways of adapting to inconvenience.

Dr. Jonathan Bricker, of the Fred Hutchinson Cancer Research Center in Seattle, has fostered a bunch of steps we can take when confronted with a diverting enticement. His methods assist patients with lessening well-being gambles through social change.4
Distinguish the inclination or thought behind your urge: When you wind up getting occupied

become mindful of the interior trigger that is provoking you to do such. Could it be said that you are feeling restless, anxious, or perhaps ineffectively qualified for the undertaking?
Get it on paper: Bricker exhorts that you record that inclination, alongside the hour of the day and what you were doing when you felt that inner trigger. Keeping a log of interruptions will assist you with connecting ways of behaving with their inward triggers. The better you get at seeing the contemplations and sentiments that go before specific ways of behaving, the better you will become at overseeing them after some time.
Investigate the sensation: Bricker exhorts becoming inquisitive about the vibes that go before the interruption. Do you get butterflies in your stomach? A fix in your chest? Bricker suggests that you stay with that inclination before following your motivation. He suggests attempting the "leaves on a stream" technique. Envision yourself next to a stream, on which leaves tenderly float by. Place each thought and pessimistic inclination to you on one leaf and watch them float away.

Notwithstanding Bricker's means, there are a few different strategies we can use to dominate the inward triggers that lead to interruption. I detail each procedure I use in my book Indistractable: How to Control Your Attention and Choose Your Life. I'll likewise be sharing a greater amount of these strategies through my bulletin. Buy in here to ensure you don't miss more extraordinary articles.

B. Set aside a few minutes for footing. Nowadays, if you don't design your day, another person will! Without understanding how it is you need to manage your time, everything is an expected interruption. To set aside a few minutes for the things that truly matter, follow these means.

Transform your qualities into time.

Many individuals talk a decent game about what's critical to them like their families, their wellbeing, and their companions, yet with regards to focusing intently on these parts of their lives, they get diverted and don't see everything through to completion. They don't satisfy their qualities since they don't set aside a few minutes for them in their day.

Values are the characteristics of the individual you need to turn into.

Instances of values could incorporate being a contributing individual from a group, being a caring guardian, being in an even handed marriage, looking for shrewdness, dealing with your actual wellness, or being a liberal companion. Many individuals could buy into these qualities, yet without making time to live them out, they're simply vacant desires.

Timebox your timetable.

The best method for ensuring you'll set aside a few minutes for your qualities is through timeboxing. Timeboxing implies concluding what you will do and while you will do it.5 The objective is to make a layout for how to invest your energy every day, taking out all void areas in your schedule.

It doesn't make any difference what you do for however long that is what you wanted to do. Feel free to look at online entertainment, however at the time you put away for it — not to the detriment of different things you intended to do, such as investing energy with your loved ones.

Conclude how long you need to dedicate to every area of your life, as per your qualities. Ensure that you plan sufficient time for yourself and your connections. All things considered, the main individuals in your day-to-day existence merit better compared to the extra opportunity in your day.

Then, make a week-by-week schedule layout for your ideal week. You can track down a free clear layout and instrument here. Then, incorporate 15 minutes out of every week to reflect and refine your schedule. Ask yourself: When did I do what I said I could do, and when did I get diverted?

If you become occupied, note the trigger and conclude what methodology you will utilize the following time it emerges.

Likewise, inquire: Are there transforms I can make to my schedule that will give me the time I have to more readily communicate my qualities?

This offers you the chance to change things that will make your schedule simpler to continue in the following week.

Synchronize with Stakeholders.

Since you have your optimal week-after-week format, now is the right time to ensure the notable individuals in your day-to-day existence are in synchronization.

Plunk down with your family and ensure you're adjusted on how you mean to invest your energy.

Try to examine who will deal with which family obligations and when you'll possess some energy for the sake of entertainment together.

At work, explain with your associates how you plan to spend your week of work so there are no curve balls. A speedy gathering to go over your timetable is a quick and profoundly powerful method for adjusting assumptions about how you'll invest your energy.

Few out of every odd organization has a corporate culture that regards individuals' time. I examine the reason why interruption is in many cases a side effect of a broken working environment, and how to fix it, in my book Indistractable: How to Control Your Attention and Choose Your Life.

C. Hack Back External Triggers.
Tech organizations utilize outer triggers to hack our considerations. The pings and dings from our gadgets frequently occupy us by pulling us from what we truly need to do. We might

attempt to disregard those triggers, yet research shows that overlooking a call or message can be similarly as diverting as answering one.6

Not all outside triggers are interruptions, nonetheless. Assuming that used to assist you with achieving errands, outside triggers can remind you to do what you arranged. While by definition there is no such thing as a decent interruption for uneasiness, an outer trigger that reminds us to have some time off can act as a redirection that has been displayed to ease actual torment or assist with controlling undesirable desires.

The right methodology is to find out if the outer trigger is serving you, or are you serving it. If the brief leads you to foot, keep it. Assuming it drives you to interruption, kill it.

Hack back your cell phone.

Whether it is in touch with family, exploring in and out of town, or paying attention to book recordings, this marvel gadget in your pocket has become key. It can likewise be a significant wellspring of interruption, however, you can reclaim your PDA in four stages:

Eliminate the applications you never again need.
Eliminate applications that you like, yet that you can use on your PC all things being equal.
Revise the excess applications on your telephone to lessen visual clutter.7
Change your warning settings for each application.
Hack Back Your Feeds.

With regards to interruption, virtual entertainment assumes an immense part. Locals like Twitter, Instagram, and Reddit are intended to send you perpetual outside triggers. Facebook's endless parchment is especially shrewd, yet you don't need to succumb to it. A few new instruments are accessible that either wipe out the news source (News Feed Eradicator) or open it solely after you've done other, more significant undertakings (Todobook).

These devices work across a few stages, permitting you to utilize applications in the manner in which you need them, as opposed to how their organizations need them. (For a greater amount of my number one instruments for hacking back, see here).

D. Forestall interruption with settlements.
The counteractant to impulsivity is thinking ahead. The last procedure for becoming indestructible is to make a "precommitment" — eliminating a future decision — to defeat distraction.8
Instances of precommitments incorporate high-level medical services mandates, retirement accounts that punish us for early withdrawal, and "together forever" marriage promises.

They are choices we concrete well ahead of the allurements and interruption we know could come. Accordingly, this step ought to just be taken after we have followed the other three stages and figured out how to deal with our inside triggers, set aside a few minutes for footing, and hacked back the outside sets off that pull us to interruptions.

There are three kinds of agreements.

A work settlement is a sort of precommitment that includes expanding how much exertion is expected to do something you would rather not do. Adding extra exertion drives you to inquire as to whether an interruption is truly worth the effort and typically you conclude that it isn't. There are various applications intended to assist you with putting forth attempt agreements with your computerized gadgets. (Genuine models incorporate SelfControl, Forest, and Freedom, however, there are numerous others.)

A cost settlement risks cash. Assuming that you adhere to your expected way of behaving, you keep the money. Assuming that you get diverted, you relinquish your assets. This sort of procedure has had surprising outcomes when used to help smokers quit.9 I utilized a value settlement to complete the main draft of my book, promising my responsibility accomplice $10,000 on the off chance that I didn't complete the draft by my cutoff time. I kept my cash and wrapped up composing my book.

At long last, a character agreement is one more method for changing your reaction to interruptions. Your mental self-view significantly affects your way of behaving. By taking on another character, you enable yourself to settle on choices in light of who you accept you are. Consider how individuals who refer to themselves as "veggie lovers" don't need to exhaust a lot of determination to try not to eat meat.

To become indestructible, you can quit letting yourself know you are an individual with a "limited capacity to focus" or an "habit-forming character" and on second thought tell yourself, "I'm indestructible." If you let yourself know you are a quickly flustered, sort of individual, it immediately turns out to be valid. In any case, assuming you accept that you are indestructible, you enable yourself to answer all the more strongly to anything that interruptions get in your way.10

Values are the traits of the individual you need to turn into.

We Can Do This

Becoming distractable isn't some puzzling recipe, it's just about as simple as following four stages. Dominating your inward triggers, setting aside a few minutes for footing, hacking back your outside triggers, and forestalling interruptions with settlements, are useful assets that can reshape your life.

The world is parting into two kinds of individuals: the people who permit their consideration and their lives to be controlled by others, and the people who gladly call themselves distractable.

At the point when you become distractable, you impact others to do likewise. You can impact partners and colleagues to attempt these procedures. You can move your loved ones to seek after the lives they imagine. You can assist your kids with realizing what makes certain to be the expertise of the hundred years, the ability to become distractable.

Chapter Eight: investigate your mentality

computer programmer versus developer
Investigating is basic expertise. More significant than the ability is the mentality. The debugger's outlook is the disposition that you should continuously figure out the why behind an issue; any ambiguities or questions are unsatisfactory. This outlook can convey you from investigating little capabilities to tackling troublesome hierarchical issues.

The Virtuous Cycle Of Debugging and Understanding
There is a prudent cycle between investigating a program and grasping a program. 95% of the time, you'll be adding to a previous codebase. To roll out rational improvements to a vault with a

long history and various creators, you want to set forth energy to figure out the framework.

A reliable approach to extending your comprehension is through investigating. Each time you squash a bug, you comprehend the framework somewhat better. When you comprehend the framework somewhat better, you are enabled to troubleshoot bigger issues. When you tackle bigger issues, you start to figure out further subtleties of the code. This makes a high-minded cycle where both your investigating abilities and your cognizance expand on one another.

This prudent cycle is your main choice. On the off chance that you neglect to investigate a little issue, you have neglected to comprehend a perused region of the code. Without a fundamental comprehension of the framework, you'll miss the mark on help structures for any further comprehension. As the framework advances, you will find it increasingly hard to keep up.

Be Scientific About It

Troubleshooting is a science. It's not speculation. It's not tossing log explanations in arbitrary areas. To troubleshoot successfully, you want a technique. Your activities should be conscious, your speculations should be demonstrated (or disproven), and you should decisively show up at arrangements.

Assuming you work closely with experienced engineers, you might get the feeling that they can normally and easily troubleshoot anything. You might feel that they work by instinct as opposed to science. It's challenging to pinpoint why their strategies are so powerful. How is this possible?

This "instinct" is simply insight. In the wake of putting long stretches of coding added to your repertoire, you will start to use previous encounters to track down heuristics in troubleshooting. You'll see a similar issue manifest itself across many tasks. This instinct is the perfection of years spent purposefully crushing bugs.

Troubleshooting Has Its Scope
Troubleshooting a bug in application code is different from troubleshooting a confounded disseminated framework. Like your undertakings, troubleshooting has to change levels of extension.

At the point when you initially begin troubleshooting, you will start by fixing issues in your neighborhood space. This may be checking for an additional edge case or forestalling a specific runtime exemption. If you're doing this consistently, soon you begin troubleshooting bigger issues.

As you acquire insight, you will start to compartmentalize data. You'll move explicit modules into secret elements, each with its particular information sources and results. You will start to zero in on connection points and combinations. You will skim through executions, just removing a more profound look from interest.

With a developing degree of mental association, the extent of your troubleshooting skills will increment. You'll have the option to perform interaction of end across different potential outcomes reliably. You'll have the option to segregate issues into explicit modules rapidly. Above all, you'll have the option to offer powerful, useful answers for the framework.

Investigating across differing extensions doesn't mean you just get to troubleshoot enormous scope issues as you become more experienced. You should be prepared to troubleshoot any issue, whether that be an edge case in a muddled circulated convention or a couple of defective lines of code.

Troubleshooting Skills Extend into Organization Problems

Your troubleshooting abilities will stretch out to various areas. A debugger's mentality can give you a more refined item sense, help you with administrative obligations, and, surprisingly, empower you to further develop business results. Regardless of which bearing you choose to direct your profession, investigating is basic.

For instance, if you go down the designing supervisor's way, there will be times when you want to troubleshoot a useless group. Like a product imperfection, you should be logical and analyze why the group isn't working great. The venture may be missing satisfactory item determination, or maybe two colleagues are clashing. As a supervisor, you should troubleshoot a hierarchical issue with the very mentality that you handle programming bugs. This implies going to additional gatherings, perusing quarrelsome code surveys, or finding the opportunity to talk with engineers. It's an alternate sort of investigating, yet it's troubleshooting.

End
The debugger's attitude is vital. You should constantly comprehend the "why" behind any

issue; anything less is inadmissible. This mentality will empower you to tackle various issues, continually build up your comprehension, and permit you to execute powerful arrangements. Concerning your profession, these abilities will help you from taking care of edge cases in capabilities to breaking down nuanced framework disappointments to fixing hierarchical shortcomings.

www.ingramcontent.com/pod-product-compliance
Lightning Source LLC
Chambersburg PA
CBHW050004230526
45465CB00003BB/1253